Sharing God's Word for Children through Cat ~~Tails~~ Tales

I0108440

"For God so loved the world ...." John 3: 16

Dedication

This book is dedicated to
the many loving, selfless individuals and agencies who share
my love and passion for rescuing animals from danger...
bringing them to a place of safety... and for restoring
their lives with happiness, peace, and hope.

ACKNOWLEDGMENTS

First and foremost, I am thankful to God for the opportunity to be of service to others and to make a difference in the lives of animals, children and youth.

Next, I am humbly grateful to my parents for their love and guidance throughout my life. I was raised in a Christian home where I learned core values such as working hard, being kind to others, taking care of those in need, telling the truth, and giving of myself to make the world a better place. Without parents committed to being honorable role models, I might not have learned these important life lessons that I still hold dear today.

Message to Parents

Dear Parent(s):

If there has ever been a need to return to core principles and virtues, the time is now. We are amid great division in our country where people have lost the basic rules of respect for one another. We witness crime and hatred every time we turn on the television or radio. Can we simply turn these off and hope to change things? For certain, we know that ignoring problems does not mean that they cease to exist.

With this fervent concern for children today and for our beloved country in the future, I encourage you to join me in reclaiming Christian values and some of the moralities that made us better. Better people. Better citizens. My hope is that today's children learn these traditional values, practice them, and live them as they become tomorrow's America.

As a former teacher of special-needs students, I have a passion and heart for serving others. Out of my love for children and my dedication to animal rescue, I have written a series of books using an animal theme centered around common virtues that will help children to be better citizens and leaders of integrity in the future.

Each book portrays a righteous virtue from the protagonist of the series, Leonardo, one of my rescued cats. He plays the role of a whimsical, **cat**erwauling clergyman!

As you read the stories, you will see why Leonardo is so special to me and why he so graciously earns this title. The books are designed to be fun and interactive so that you can read them with your children and have discussion about each virtue.

Vocabulary words that you will need to explain to your children are in bold font and there is a glossary and an activity page at the end of each book for your children to enjoy.

Thank you for allowing me to come into your homes in this magical way. My prayers are with you and your children!

Warmest regards,

Sherry Lynn Dowis, Ph.D.

Help for a Little Kitten!

As I made my way down a busy
highway, I noticed a tiny squirrel **hunkered** down
in the middle of the road– cars zooming
around it left and right!

As I approached closer, I realized it
wasn't a squirrel but a tiny, little kitten with a
badly hurt leg.

I immediately found a place to turn around and drove back to the **stranded** critter hoping to save it from a very tragic ending.

I parked in the cement
median with two lanes of cars to
my right and two to my left.

As soon as there was a break in traffic, I scooted to the **abandoned** and **injured** kitty. He had sensed my **mercy** and began dragging his leg and tiny little body to meet me.

In all my years of animal rescue,
I have never witnessed such pure **despair**, yet
such longing to survive.

He knew I was there to help him!

His eyes met mine, and ....

at that very moment, we became .....

Soul Mates.

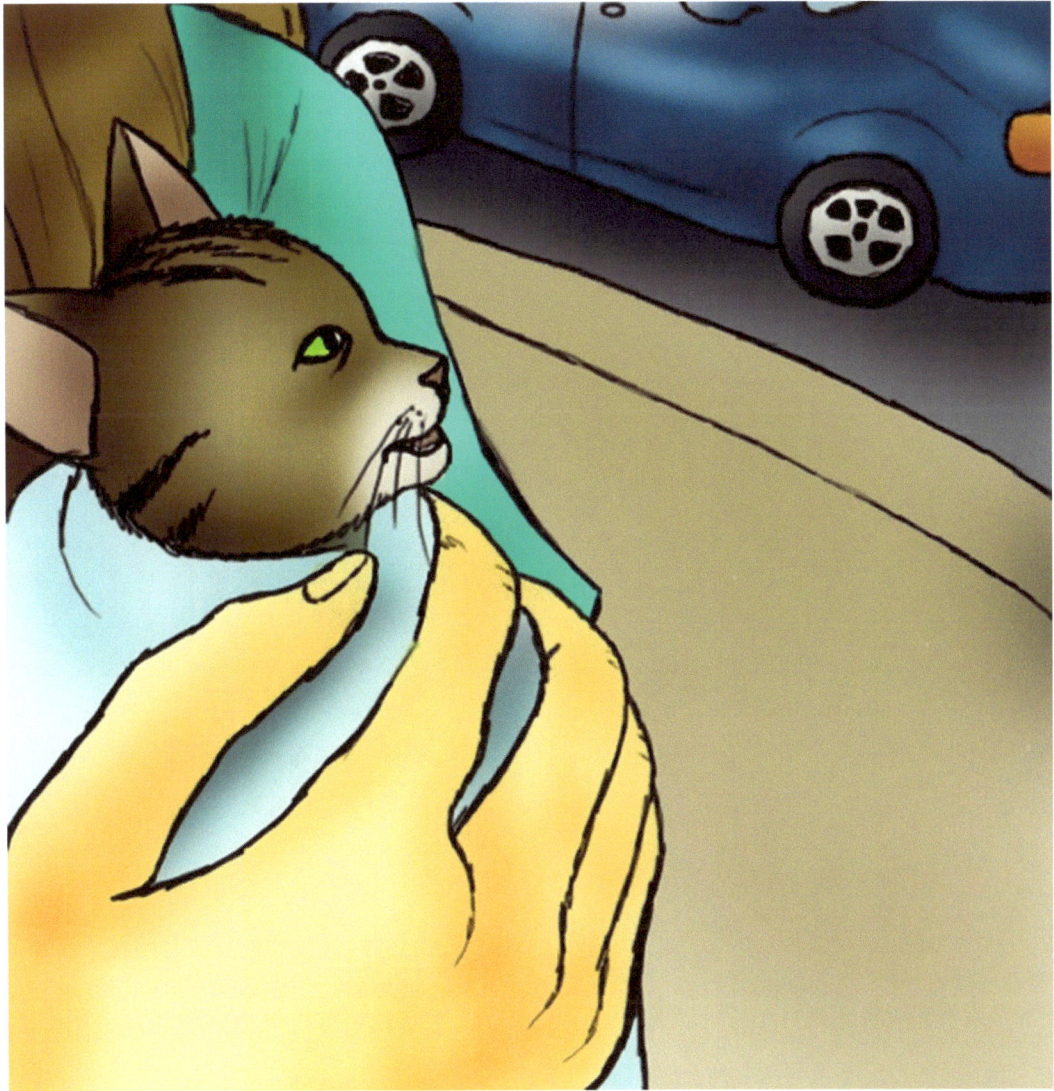

Traffic was quickly approaching so I had
no time to spare. I scooped him up and
made a dash back to the median to get
him safely in my car.

All of a sudden, the noisy, zooming
traffic scared the kitten. He jumped out of
my hands and hid underneath my car!

Without thinking and out of sheer **panic**, I got on my hands and knees and scooted myself under the car enough to grab him with one hand.

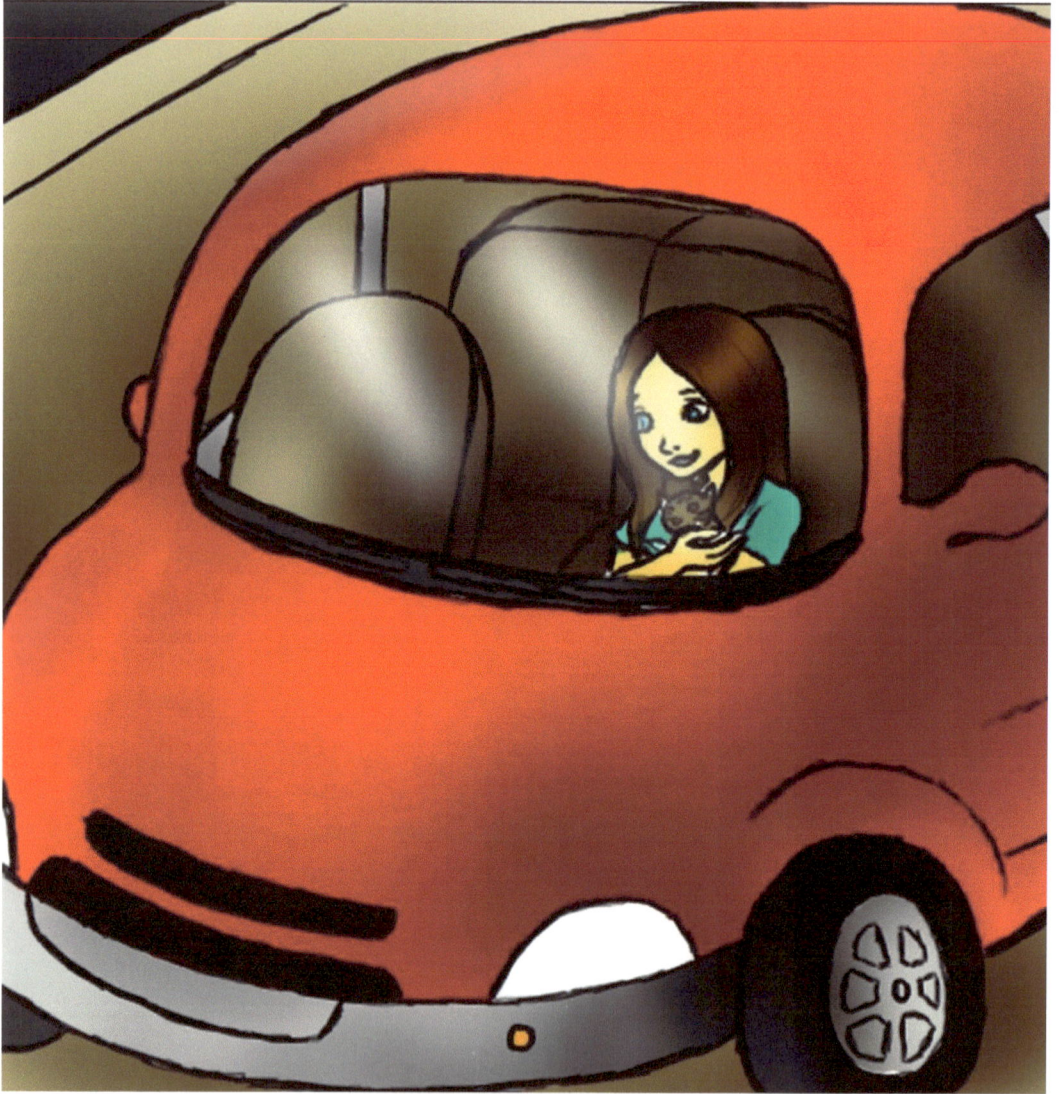

Thankfully, I had him **in tow**. I jumped in the car with him and just sat there with my heart still **pounding** out of my chest.

I expected him to **moan** and cry from his
injured leg, but he didn't. All in all,
he seemed fine! He fell fast asleep
in my lap as I continued to drive.

As soon as possible, I took him to the emergency hospital for animals. The doctor gave him a thorough examination. The **veterinarian** was very nice and Leonardo was brave!

Unfortunately, the injured leg had to be **amputated**. This means his leg was removed. But don't worry! Leonardo was asleep with medicine and did not feel any pain.

The name, Leonardo, means: strong lion, unstoppable…. and natural winner. Every day, Leonardo lives up to his name. With his bold **enthusiasm** for LIFE, I decided that he is Leonardo ……   the three-legged, **CATerwauling** Clergyman!!

Sermon 1:
Being Relentless

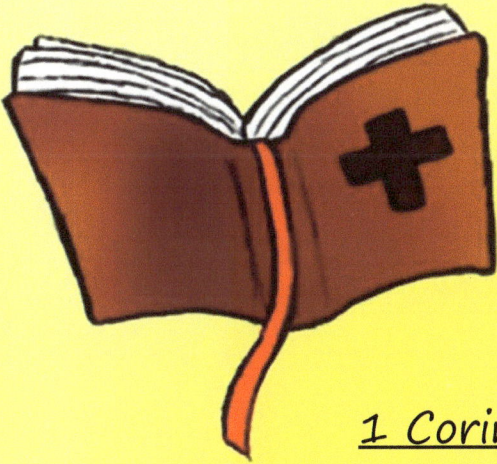

1 Corinthians 15:58

"Therefore, my dear brothers, stand firm. Let nothing move you. Always give yourselves fully to the work of the Lord, because you know that your labor in the Lord is not in vain."

When Leonardo came home from the animal hospital he was in a room all by himself so that his brother and sister cats could not hurt him.

He could see them through a glass door and
he wanted to play with them SO much!
He would mew at them ...
and even tried to open the door with his paw.

I had to give him all kinds of toys to
play with, so he would not get bored.
He scooted around on the floor, kicked balls
of yarn under the table ...

and even batted at small, stuffed toys that were shaped like mice!

Leonardo was **relentless**! This means that he was **persistent** and never gave up! He had a positive attitude and never fussed or complained about losing his leg.

Leonardo's message for us is to be relentless in our faith and in our daily living. God wants us to always DO our best and BE our best.

God watches over us from Heaven and it makes him happy when we work hard and have a positive attitude…. just like Leonardo!

Even when our work is hard or when
our life is not fun or easy..... NEVER give up!
God sees our work and will reward us
someday when we get to Heaven.

Glossary

<u>Hunkered</u> – kneeling closely down; hunched down (to be taking shelter).

<u>Stranded</u> – to be left alone and helpless.

<u>Median</u> – the middle part of the highway between lanes of traffic.

<u>Abandoned</u> – to be alone and deserted; cast aside.

<u>Injured</u> – hurt; harmed or damaged.

<u>Mercy</u> – a blessing; protection from harm

<u>Despair</u> – complete loss of hope; discouraged; very unhappy.

<u>Soul mates</u> – close friends joined by the heart and one's spirit.

<u>Panic</u> – sudden fear or anxiety.

<u>In tow</u> – in one's control; held; secured in hand.

<u>Pounding</u> – heaving beating and throbbing.

<u>Moan</u> – a long, low cry to show hurt or pain.

<u>Veterinarian</u> – a doctor for animals.

<u>Amputated</u> – cut off or removed by surgery (by a doctor).

<u>Enthusiasm</u> – lots of joy and excitement.

Caterwauling – howling or screaming.

Relentless – to never quit; continuing; unstoppable.

Persistent – determined; steady; continuing for a long, period of time.

....

Write down any other words with which you need help to understand:

_____

_____

_____

_____

_____

ACTIVITY CENTER

1.   L N E R T E S L S E

   Unscramble the letters above to spell today's word:

   _____

2.   What does today's word mean?

   _____

   _____

3.   Think of a time when you have been relentless and refused to give up.

_____

_____

Draw a picture here.

4. See if you can find these words hidden in the puzzle:

HEAVEN	JESUS	BLESS
HAPPY	NEVER	GIVE
LEONARDO	GOD	UP
RELENTLESS	WORK HARD	LOVE

```
S G M O D R A H K R O W V
S W I D C P Y Z D U E I J
E E A V E N P P O F L K E
L C N U E I P H G X E Q S
T D L V J L A F E G N S U
N O E T U K H B E A T P S
E R T H J I S X K L V R W
L E O F S O D R A N O E L
E L B T E O P C X Y T V N
R T Y S S E L B H M T R E
```

ABOUT THE AUTHOR

Born and raised in the small, Southern town of Ninety Six, South Carolina, I am a down-to-earth person. I have always remained close to my roots and have a deep appreciation for the simple things in life. I am also devoted to my family and friends and love spending time with them.

I am a retired educator with thirty-two years in the field of special education. Throughout my career, I taught students with intellectual, learning and emotional disabilities and eventually became a school district administrator in special education.

Keeping active in life and in education, I currently serve as an adjunct professor at the college level where I teach course work in special education and school administration/supervision. I also provide training and professional development to school districts regarding services and instruction to students with disabilities.

I currently reside in Sandy Springs which is part of the township of Pendleton in the upstate region of South Carolina. In my spare time, I enjoy playing the piano, reading, spending time with my family, and taking care of my ten rescued pets!

Leonardo